"The African Tribe Of Jewish Decent"

Igbo and the Jewish trajectory

A tale of two nations connected by history

Kendrick Callaway

Copyright

Table of contents

Chapter One

THE IGBO STORY

The Nri people of Igbo nation have a creation myth that is one of the many creation myths that exist in different parts of Igbo societies. The Nri and Aguleri people are in the territory of the Umueri clan, who trace their descent to the patriarchal royal figure Eri. Eri's origin is unclear, although he has been described as a "celestial being" sent by Chukwu (God). It has been characterized as the first to give the people of Anambra the social order. Historian Elizabeth Allo Isichei says, "Nri and Aguleri and part of the Umueri clan are an assemblage of Igbo village groups who trace their origins to a heaven called Eri."

Archaeological evidence suggests that Nri influence in Igboland may date back to the 9th century, and royal burials dating to at least the 10th century have been discovered. Eri, the god-like founder of Nri, is said to have settled in the region around 948, followed by other related Igbo cultures in the 13th century. The first Eze Nri (King of Nri) Ìfikuánim followed him directly. According to Igbo oral tradition, his reign began in 1043. At least one historian places the reign of Ìfikuánim much later, around 1225 AD.

Each king traces their lineage back to the founding ancestor Eri. Each king is a ritual reproduction of Eri. The initiation rite of a new king shows that the ritual process of becoming Ezenri (Nri Priest-King) closely follows the path followed by the hero in establishing the Nri Kingdom.

The Kingdom of Nri was a religious state, a type of theocratic state, that developed in the central heartland of the Igbo region. The Nri had seven types of taboos, including human (like giving birth to twins), animal (like killing or eating pythons), object, time, behavior, language, and place taboos. The rules regarding these taboos were used to educate and govern Nri's subjects. This meant that while certain Igbo may have lived under a different formal administration, all followers of the Igbo religion had to abide by the precepts of the faith and obey their representative on earth, the Eze Nri.

Traditional Igbo Society

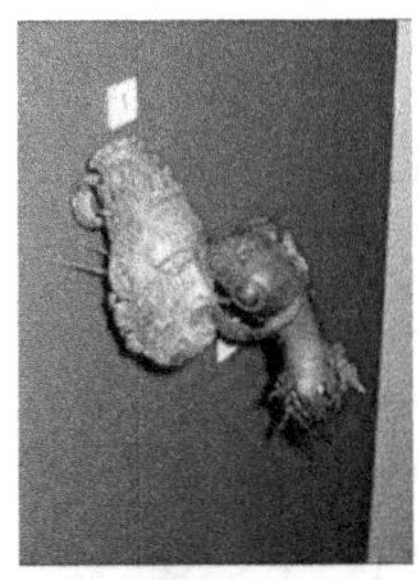

Bronze from the ninth century town of Igbo Ukwu, now at the British Museum.

The traditional Igbo political organization was based on a quasi-democratic republican system of government. In close-knit communities, this system guaranteed its citizens equality, in contrast to a feudal system with a king ruling over the subjects. This system of government was witnessed by the Portuguese, who first arrived and met with the Igbo people in the 15th century. With the exception of some notable Igbo cities like Onitsha, which had kings named Obi, and places like the Nri kingdom and Arochukwu, which had priest-kings; Igbo communities and territorial governments were predominantly governed by a republican consultative assembly of common people. Communities were usually governed and administered by a council of elders.

Although titulars were respected for their accomplishments and skills, they were not revered as kings, but often performed special functions bestowed upon them by such assemblies. This way of governing differed from most other communities in West Africa and was shared only by the ewes of Ghana. Umunna are a form of patrilineage maintained by the Igbo people. The law begins with the Umunna, a male lineage from a founding ancestor (after whom the lineage is sometimes named) with groups of compounds containing closely related families headed by the eldest male member. The Umunna can be considered the most important pillar of Igbo society. It was also a culture in which gender was reconstructed and performed according to social needs; "The flexibility of Igbo sex construction meant that sex was separate from biological sex. Daughters could become sons and consequently male.

The math in indigenous Igbo society is evident in their calendar, banking system, and strategic gambling game called okwe. In their indigenous calendar, a week had four days, a month consisted of seven weeks, and a year had 13 months. An additional day was added in the last month. This calendar is still used in indigenous Igbo villages and towns to determine market days. They settled legal matters through mediators, and their banking system for loans and savings, called Isusu, is also still in use. The Igbo New Year, which begins with the month Ọnwạ Mbụ (Igbo: First Moon), occurs in the third week of February, although the traditional beginning of the year for many Igbo communities is around spring in Ọnwạ Ágwụ (June). Used as a ceremonial script by secret societies, the Igbo have an indigenous ideographic set of symbols called Nsibidi, derived from the neighboring Ejagham people.

Igbo people were making bronzes as early as the 9th century, some of which have been found in the town of Igbo Ukwu in Anambra state.

A system of indentured servitude existed among the Igbo before and after their encounter with Europeans. Indentured service in Igbo areas was described by Olaudah Equiano in his memoirs. He describes the conditions of slaves in his Essaka community and points out the difference between the treatment of slaves among the Igbo of Essaka and those in the care of Europeans in the West Indies:

...but how different was their condition from that of the slaves of the West Indies! With us they work no more than other members of the community... even their master; ...(except that they were not allowed to eat with these...freeborns ;) and there was little other difference between them,...Some of these slaves have...slaves under them as their own property...for their own Use.

The coast of Niger was the scene of contact between European merchants and the local African kingdoms from 1434 with the arrival of the Portuguese. Portuguese slave traders set up factories and began buying enslaved local Africans and shipping them across the Atlantic to their colonies in the Americas, particularly Brazil. Slave traders from other European nations soon followed, and the region became an important hub of the Atlantic slave trade. European involvement in the Atlantic slave trade was gradually banned during the 19th century, and as such, Europeans in the region began to shift their focus away from trade and towards colonialism. Before European contact, Igbo trade routes extended as far as Mecca, Medina and Jeddah in the African continent and the Middle East.

Chapter Two

THE JEWISH STORY

The history of the early Jews focuses on the Fertile Crescent and the east coast of the Mediterranean. It begins with those people who inhabited the area between the Nile and Mesopotamia. Surrounded by ancient cultural sites in Egypt and Babylonia, the deserts of Arabia, and the highlands of Asia Minor, the land of Canaan (roughly equivalent to modern Israel, the Palestinian territories, Jordan, and Lebanon) was a meeting place of civilizations.

The earliest recorded evidence of a people called Israel appears in the Merneptah stele of ancient Egypt, which dates to around 1200 BC. According to the modern archaeological record, the Israelites and their culture branched out from the Canaanite peoples and their cultures through the development of a distinctly monolatristic—and later monotheistic—religion centered on the national god Yahweh. They spoke an archaic form of the Hebrew language now known as Biblical Hebrew.

The traditional religious view of Jews and Judaism on their own history was based on the narrative of the ancient Hebrew Bible. In this view, Abraham means that he is both the biological progenitor of the Jews and the father of Judaism, the first Jew. Later, Isaac was born of Abraham and Jacob was born of Isaac. After a battle with an angel, Jacob was given the name Israel. After a severe drought, Jacob and his twelve sons fled to Egypt, where they eventually formed the Twelve Tribes of Israel. The Israelites were later led out of slavery in Egypt and then taken to Canaan by Moses; finally they conquered Canaan under the leadership of Joshua.

Modern scholars agree that the Bible does not provide an authentic account of the origins of the Israelites; The consensus supports that the archaeological evidence, showing largely indigenous origins of Israel in Canaan rather than Egypt, is "overwhelming" and leaves "no room for either an exodus from Egypt or a 40-year pilgrimage through the Sinai wilderness." Many archaeologists have abandoned the archaeological study of Moses and the Exodus as "a fruitless quest." A century of research by archaeologists and Egyptologists has arguably found no evidence linking directly to the Exodus narrative of an Egyptian captivity and escape and journeys through the wilderness, leading to the assumption that Iron Age Israel was the Kingdoms of Judah and Israel was - originated in Canaan, not Egypt: the culture of the earliest Israelite settlements is Canaanite, their cult objects are that of the Canaanite god El, the pottery remains in the local Canaanite tradition, and the alphabet used is ancient Canaanite. Almost the only feature that distinguishes the "Israelite" villages from Canaanite sites is the absence of pig bones, although whether this can be considered an ethnic feature or is due to other factors remains a matter of debate.

However, it is accepted that this narrative has a "historical core".

According to the biblical narrative, the land of Israel was organized into a confederation of twelve tribes ruled by a series of judges for several hundred years.

Kingdoms of Israel and Judah

During Iron Age II, two Israelite kingdoms emerged: Israel and Judah. The Bible presents Israel and Judah as successors to an earlier United Kingdom of Israel, although its historicity is disputed. Historians and archaeologists agree that the northern kingdom of Israel was founded around 900 BC. 700 BC: 169–195 and that the kingdom of Judah The Tel Dan stele, discovered in 1993, shows that the kingdom existed in at least some form as early as the mid-ninth century B.C.

Biblical tradition says that the Israelite monarchy ended in 1037 B.C. It was founded under Saul and continued under David and his son Solomon. David greatly expanded the kingdom's borders and conquered Jerusalem from the Jebusites, making it the national, political, and religious capital of the kingdom. Solomon and his son later built the first temple on Mount Moriah in Jerusalem. After his death, traditionally dated c. 930 BC Civil war broke out between the ten northern Israelite tribes and the southern tribes of Judah (Simeon was absorbed into Judah) and Benjamin. The kingdom then split into the kingdom of Israel to the north and the kingdom of Judah to the south.

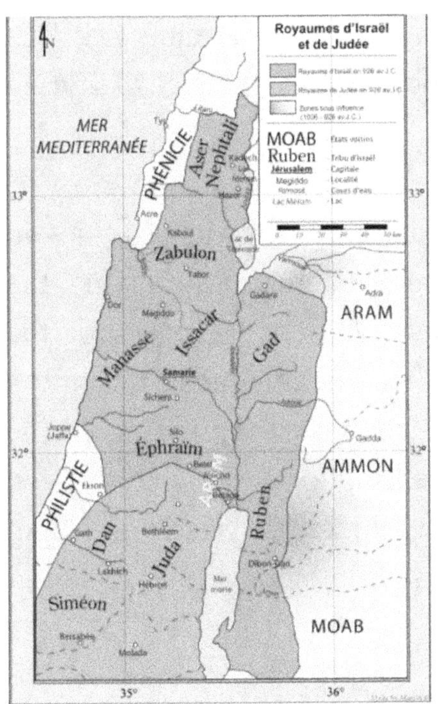

Kingdoms of Israel and Judah in 926BCE

The Kingdom of Israel was the wealthier of the two kingdoms and soon became a regional power. During the time of the Omrid dynasty, it controlled Samaria, Galilee, the upper Jordan Valley, the Sharon and much of Transjordan. Samaria, the capital, was home to one of the largest Iron Age palaces in the Levant. The

Kingdom of Israel was founded around 720 BC. destroyed when conquered by the Neo-Assyrian Empire.

The Kingdom of Judah, with its capital in Jerusalem, controlled the Judean Mountains, the Shephelah, the Judean Desert and parts of the Negev. After the fall of Israel, Judah became a vassal state of the Neo-Assyrian Empire. In the 7th century B.C. The kingdom's population grew rapidly and prospered under Assyrian vassalage, despite Hezekiah's revolt against the Assyrian king Sennacherib.

With the fall of the Neo-Assyrian Empire in 605 B.C. A contest arose between Egypt and the Neo-Babylonian Empire for control of the Levant, ultimately leading to Judah's rapid decline. In the early 6th century B.C. A wave of Egyptian-backed Judean rebellions against Babylonian rule was crushed. 586 BC King Nebuchadnezzar II of Babylon conquered Judah and destroyed Jerusalem and the first temple.

The kingdom's elite and many of their people were exiled to Babylon, where religion developed outside of the traditional temple. Others fled to Egypt. The defeat was also recorded in the Babylonian chronicles.

Chapter Three

THE IGBO AND JEWISH CONNECTION

In recent decades, several Igbo have migrated to Israel, most notably to Tel Aviv. This wave of immigration can be explained in part by a small diaspora established in Israel with Nigeria's independence in 1960. This is partly due to extensive educational programs that the Israelis implemented in the new Nigerian state after the 1960s, introducing many people for the first time to the idea of Israel as a modern nation-state and the possible opportunities that existed for the Jews living there.

The Igbo Jewish community is not recognized by the Supreme Court of Israel as a Jewish community for the purpose of immigrating to Israel. Additionally, none of the mainstream denominations of Judaism consider the group to be an authentically Jewish community. Although they identify as part of the worldwide Jewish community, they still struggle to be recognized as Jews by other Jews. A member of the Gihon Hebrews synagogue expressed this struggle to Shai Afsai in Abuja: "We say we are Jews by blood. We're locked out now; we can't go anywhere and participate as Jews. not excluded and isolated from other Jews."

However, some Igbo Jews are currently adopting stricter religious customs to gain more acceptance in the mainstream Jewish community. Daniel Lis explained in his article that parts of the Igbo Jewish community are conforming to the standards of orthodox Judaism in order to be generally accepted as Jews in Israel.

While Igbo Jews claim that they are the descendants of ancient Israelites, others say they lack historical evidence that would prove their descent from such a community, and also lack evidence of continuous practice of Judaism that predates the should lie in colonial contact. Regardless of the historicity of their claims, the Igbo Jews can easily be recognized as modern Jews either by the State of Israel as a whole or by one of the major currents of Jewish religion, giving them automatic recognition by the State of Israel. The possibility that the state could make such a decision, and the possibility of a Jewish denomination recognizing the entire community as authentically Jewish, is thwarted by the fact that some Igbo Jews simultaneously claim to be Christians by declaring their denomination to Judaism and their beliefs, claims to have a Jewish identity called into question. Among them are some Igbo who immigrated to Israel illegally, claiming to be Jews and Christians at the same time. According to the official Israeli administration, a number of Igbo people have been granted the right to travel to Israel for the purpose of Christian pilgrimage, but they have overstayed their visas and are now living and working in the country illegally.

The State of Israel has not made any official recommendations as to whether the Igbo Jews constitute a legally recognized Jewish community for the purpose of immigrating to Israel, nor is their legal status currently discussed at any level within the State. However, several Igbo Jews who formally converted to Orthodox or Conservative Judaism have been accepted as Jews on an individual basis under the Law of Return, and they have also immigrated to Israel.

According to Eze Obidiegwu Onyesoh, the traditional ruler of Nri, a man named Eri, the progenitor of Ndigbo, lived in Egypt and was special adviser on religious affairs to the 5th dynasty of Egyptian pharaohs.

In those days in Egypt, Eri determined who would be the next pharaoh. And by their law there was a deity named Emem, and everything that happened during that time was the responsibility of the man named Eri, in his capacity as religious adviser to the pharaoh of Egypt.

Now Eri needed people to help him and he recruited devotees. These devotees were all appointed by him, but he had to do something to really find their own allegiance. Moving towards the south side, they reached another confluence. This confluence was the tributary of the Niger and Benue rivers, known as the Ezu na Omambala.

Eri's last son, Agulu, stayed by the sea because he was a fisherman. The first child Eri stayed in his father's house until he had a vision and was called to serve God in his own way. Nri was an incarnation of his grandfather Eri.

Thus, Nri was the reincarnation of Eri, and the functions that her grandfather performed traced back to him. While his siblings all went to their respective farming positions, he stayed on his father's grounds. The Ofo Ndigbo reside in Nri because the process is from one Eze-Nri to another. There is a surrender known as Ofo and Alo and to become Eze-Nri without the original Ofo and Alo you are not Eze Nri. The Ofo and Alo have been around for 1,009 years.

When I finish and leave as Eze Nri, Ofo and Alo are passed to the next Eze Nri.

Today about 180 communities can trace their origin from Nri and Nri civilization spread. He established the Ozo title just like his father; He spoke about everything to do with fairness and justice. Everywhere he founded in his grandfather's name they called themselves Igbo.

He added: Aguleri, the last born of Eri, stayed very close to the waterfront. Aguleri cannot claim that Nri came from Aguleri. Nri came from a place called Eriaka and Eriaka is deceased for now because the captain left Eriaka.

Eze Nri, Onyesoh said, does not go to Aguleri to be crowned or purified, adding that as part of the tradition, after being crowned and other things perfected, Eze Nri must go where water is divided in two be. He continued: We have no other two-part water like Lokoja, the confluence of the Niger and Benue. The place is too far for us and the nearest to us is the tributary of the Niger and Benue known as the Ezu and Omambala. They have two rivers there, now it's on that river where the covenant has to be made. This bond is what we know as "Udu-Eze".

Any person who tells you that Eze-Nri has to go to Aguleri for anything else is lying. Apart from the distance, one could also go to converging places between Niger and Benue to perform the rite instead of going to Aguleri. So any kind of propaganda you hear now is all fabric of lies.

Nri does not have a culture similar to that of Aguleri. It has not had a traditional institution since the early days of Aguleri.

If Nri and Aguleri have much in common, Aguleri would produce her own traditional ruler just like Nri. For the past 110 years it has only been the Idigo dynasty that has held the kingship.

Image of Jewish Igbos.

Igbo Jewish girls dancing and singing outside their synagogue.

An Igbo mother and her son.

Relationship between the Holocaust and Igbo genocide

One to three million people died during the massacre of Igbos in Nigeria between 1966 and 1970. In the decades since, writers have labored to understand the immense human tragedy.

These literary accounts of the massacres use the Holocaust as an important point of reference.

The war in Nigeria, with its attendant mass atrocities, is arguably one of the first major moments in post-colonial Africa in which allegations of genocide were raised. Following military coups in Nigeria in 1966, military and ethnic extremists systematically attacked and killed Igbos in what was then Nigeria's northern and western regions.

Massacres of Igbos and other Easterners across the country left thousands dead and displaced millions.

The massacres prompted the eastern region of Nigeria to declare secession. The region was renamed the Republic of Biafra. Nigeria invaded Biafra in July 1967, resulting in a protracted war. The federal government employed starvation tactics that resulted in more than three million civilian deaths in Biafra. Biafra officially surrendered to Nigeria in January 1970.

After its genocidal war, the Nigerian government has developed a culture of denial.

To counter this propaganda, writers reflecting on this past have often referred to the war as genocide. A common feature in the scriptures is the comparison of Igbo experiences of atrocities with Jewish ones during thThee Holocaust.

Holocaust as a cultural icon of genocide

During the Biafran War, US-based Igbo poet Onwuchekwa Jemie compared the killing of Igbos in Nigeria to the Nazi killing of Jews during World War II. His poem "Requiem" (from his 1970 anthology Biafra: Requiem for the Dead in War) reflects this:

"Once in 53 three times in 66 Nigerians shoot civilians through the ears, repeat all known tortures, murder all men and rape old women, force teenage girls into leprosy clinics, hundreds are slaughtered... the 30,000 innocents are mowed down Nazi-style, a final solution, which failed again."

The lines "a final solution / that failed again" sum up the poet's defiant view that Biafra will survive the genocidal attack from Nigeria.

Global historian Lasse Heerten has explained in his work on Biafra that such comparisons of Igbo suffering to the Nazi genocide of the Jews reveal the growing awareness of the Holocaust in African conflict zones at the time.

Comparing Igbo suffering to the Holocaust offers the authors an opportunity to internationalize the Igbo experience in Nigeria. In doing so, they share a moral message about the universal condition of human cruelty.